AF489069

Pan the Tortoiseshell Cat's Big Adventure

By: Cassy M. Edwards

To my children
Sophia, Julian, & Elaina

Love,
Mom

Once upon a time, in a cozy little cottage, there lived a tortoiseshell cat named Panther. Everyone in the neighborhood called her "Pan." Pan was special because she had patches of black, orange, and cream fur that made her look like a walking work of art.

Pan had bright, curious eyes that sparkled with mischief. She loved to explore the garden and chase butterflies, but today, she felt a different kind of excitement in the air.

2

As Pan roamed the garden, she noticed a colorful butterfly with wings that shimmered like a rainbow. "Wow!" she thought. "I've never seen a butterfly like that before."

The butterfly fluttered just out of reach, leading Pan on a playful chase. "I'm going on an adventure!" she purred to herself.

Pan followed the butterfly
through the garden, past the tall
sunflowers, and under the leafy
arch of the old oak tree.

The butterfly landed on a big, mossy rock near a sparkling stream. Pan watched in wonder as it sipped nectar from a wildflower.

"Hello," Pan mewed softly. "You're the most beautiful butterfly I've ever seen. What's your name?"

The butterfly fluttered its wings
and replied, "I'm Rainbow, and I'm
on a journey to visit all the gardens
in the world. Would you like to
come along, Pan?"

Pan's heart danced with excitement.
"Yes, Rainbow! I'd love to join you
on your adventure."

9

Together, Pan and Rainbow embarked on a grand adventure. They explored meadows, climbed hills, and even met a friendly squirrel named Sam along the way.

Pan learned about the beauty
of nature, the kindness of
new friends, and the joy of
discovery.

After many days of fun, Rainbow
said, "It's time for me to continue
my journey, but you, Pan, will
always have the spirit of adventure
in your heart."

12

With a flutter of colorful wings,
Rainbow disappeared into the
sky, leaving Pan with wonderful
memories of their adventure.

13

Pan returned to her cozy cottage, where she would share her stories with her fellow feline friends and dream of new adventures to come.

14

And so, Panther, the tortoiseshell cat, discovered that even in her own backyard, there were countless adventures waiting to be explored, just like the heart of a true adventurer.

The End.

www.ingramcontent.com/pod-product-compliance
Lightning Source LLC
Chambersburg PA
CBHW040940110726
48006CB00001B/207